BETTER
CONVERSATIONS
EVERY DAY™

THE IDEAS INTO ACTION SERIES DRAWS ON THE PRACTICAL KNOWLEDGE THAT THE CENTER FOR CREATIVE LEADERSHIP (CCL)®, SINCE ITS INCEPTION IN 1970, HAS GENERATED THROUGH ITS RESEARCH AND EDUCATIONAL ACTIVITIES CONDUCTED IN PARTNERSHIP WITH HUNDREDS OF THOUSANDS OF LEADERS. MUCH OF THIS KNOWLEDGE IS SHARED—IN A WAY THAT IS DISTINCT FROM THE TYPICAL UNIVERSITY DEPARTMENT, PROFESSIONAL ASSOCIATION, OR CONSULTANCY. CCL IS NOT SIMPLY A COLLECTION OF INDIVIDUAL EXPERTS, ALTHOUGH THE INDIVIDUAL CREDENTIALS OF ITS STAFF ARE IMPRESSIVE; RATHER IT IS A COMMUNITY, WITH ITS MEMBERS HOLDING CERTAIN PRINCIPLES IN COMMON AND WORKING TOGETHER TO UNDERSTAND AND GENERATE PRACTICAL RESPONSES TO TODAY'S LEADERSHIP AND ORGANIZATIONAL CHALLENGES. THE PURPOSE OF THE SERIES IS TO PROVIDE LEADERS WITH SPECIFIC ADVICE ON HOW TO COMPLETE A DEVELOPMENTAL TASK OR SOLVE A LEADERSHIP CHALLENGE. IN DOING THAT, THE SERIES CARRIES OUT CCL'S MISSION TO ADVANCE THE UNDERSTANDING, PRACTICE, AND DEVELOPMENT OF LEADERSHIP FOR THE BENEFIT OF SOCIETY WORLDWIDE. WE THINK YOU WILL FIND THE IDEAS INTO ACTION SERIES AN IMPORTANT ADDITION TO YOUR LEADERSHIP TOOLKIT.

BETTER
CONVERSATIONS
EVERY DAY™

*4 Core Skills That
Will Change the
Way You Lead and
Live Your Life*

Maggie Sass
Andre Keil

MAGGIE SASS, PHD IS AN ORGANIZATIONAL PSYCHOLOGIST AND EXECUTIVE COACH WORKING AT THE CONVERGENCE OF DATA, EMOTIONAL INTELLIGENCE, AND LEADERSHIP DEVELOPMENT. SHE IS PASSIONATE ABOUT THE POWER OF COACHING TO TRANSFORM INDIVIDUALS' LIVES AND THE FABRIC OF TEAM AND ORGANIZATIONAL CULTURE.

AS AN EXECUTIVE LEADER OF APPLIED RESEARCH AND DEVELOPMENT AT TALENTSMARTEQ AND A FORMER COACHING SOLUTIONS PARTNER AT THE CENTER FOR CREATIVE LEADERSHIP, MAGGIE DRAWS ON HER RICH ACADEMIC BACKGROUND AND BREADTH OF EXPERIENCE IN COACHING BUT ALSO ASSESSMENT AND EVALUATION TO TRANSLATE RESEARCH INTO PRACTICAL, SCALABLE SOLUTIONS FOR CLIENTS. SHE HAS TRAINED AND COACHED LEADERS AND THEIR TEAMS WORLDWIDE FOCUSING ON SUSTAINABLE BEHAVIOR CHANGE AND REAL BUSINESS IMPACT. MAGGIE IS AN ADJUNCT PROFESSOR OF COACHING AND MENTORING AT THE CALIFORNIA SCHOOL OF PROFESSIONAL PSYCHOLOGY AND LIVES IN SAN DIEGO, CA.

ANDRE KEIL BRINGS MORE THAN 15 YEARS OF EXPERIENCE AS AN EXECUTIVE COACH IN THE LEADERSHIP-CONSULTING SPACE. HIS FOCUS IS HELPING FORTUNE 500 LEADERS RESPOND BETTER TO COMPLEX, CONTINUOUSLY CHANGING BUSINESS ENVIRONMENTS SO THEY CAN BECOME MORE EFFECTIVE, RESILIENT INDIVIDUALS IN BOTH THEIR

PROFESSIONAL AND PERSONAL LIVES. ANDRE BRINGS A
UNIQUE UNDERSTANDING OF THE VALUE OF COACHING
BOTH AS A PRACTITIONER AND AS A FORMER LEADER OF THE
CENTER FOR CREATIVE LEADERSHIP'S COACHING PRACTICE.
ANDRE IS EXPERIENCED AT DESIGNING AND IMPLEMENTING
COACHING PROGRAMS AND CREATING CONTENT THAT
MOVES THE NEEDLE FOR PROGRAM PARTICIPANTS, HAVING
WORKED WITH COUNTLESS ORGANIZATIONS ALL OVER THE
GLOBE TO CREATE CULTURES OF TRUST AND TRANSPARENCY.
ANDRE IS A FOUNDING MEMBER OF THE INTERNATIONAL
COACH FEDERATION'S TRAINING EXECUTIVE BOARD AND
RESIDES IN NORTH CAROLINA.

SPECIAL THANKS TO ANNE CREDI, GEORGE HALLENBECK,
AND STEPHANIE HAYNES FOR REVIEWING AN EARLY VERSION
OF THIS MANUSCRIPT.

WE ALSO WANT TO THANK RICH BEEN, KARA PENFIELD,
ANGELA EDWARDS, AND NICOLE FORWARD FOR THEIR
CONTRIBUTIONS TOWARDS SHAPING THE CONCEPTS OF
BETTER CONVERSATIONS EVERY DAY. LASTLY, WE HAVE
SPECIAL GRATITUDE FOR CHUCK AINSWORTH, WHO
DEVELOPED THE INITIAL BETTER CONVERSATIONS PROGRAM
AND BROUGHT IT TO COUNTLESS LEADERS ACROSS THE
WORLD.

CCL PRESS

ONE LEADERSHIP PLACE, GREENSBORO, NC 27410

©2022 CENTER FOR CREATIVE LEADERSHIP

ISBN-13: 978-1-64761-081-4 (PRINT)

ISBN-13: 978-1-64761-082-1 (EBOOK)

ISBN-13: 9781-64761-083-8 (EPDF)

CCL NO. 475

CONTENTS

NOTE TO THE READER

The Center for Creative Leadership's mission is to advance the understanding, practice, and development of leadership for the benefit of society worldwide. Our research, publications, assessment tools, and skill development programs strive to make the world a better place by teaching people from all walks of life to be better leaders. Based on our experience in working with thousands of leaders, we know that effective communication—or simply, having better conversations every day—is an foundational leadership skill. While many ideas in this book will be helpful for managers and leaders, the skills discussed in this book are universal. This book will provide practical tips, tricks, and concepts that anyone can use to communicate better, connect more deeply, build trust, and be more satisfied—inside and outside of work. Think of this guidebook as your GPS system: a tool that can help you know where to start, what to watch out for, and suggestions for ways to navigate new skills. When practiced consistently, we think the concepts in this book can end up changing your impact at work and the relationships in your life.

The Challenge
with Conversations

Think back to the conversations you've had over the last three months: Was there ever a time where you wished for a "do-over?" Or perhaps you've been avoiding a conversation with someone because every time you talk to them it leaves you feeling angry, confused, or misunderstood. Or maybe you've spent countless hours thinking and talking with everyone about a conversation you need to have, except for the actual person that you need to speak with. Many of our conversations don't always go the way we intend, which can lead to misunderstanding and confusion at best, and at worst can break down critical relationships. But done the right way, a great conversation, or just a *better* conversation, can connect you to people in productive ways, enable you to share your ideas more effectively, improve collaboration, influence decisions, and get work done with clarity and ease. And beyond the workplace, a better conversation can help you build deeper connections, trust, and relationships with your friends and family.

The Center for Creative Leadership's (CCL) research of C-suite executives has shown that communication is perceived as one of three critical competencies for effective change management, along with collaboration and commitment (Dellaert & Kernick, 2019). Much of that communication comes through conversations. These are moments of truth where you have an opportunity to make more meaningful connections with your colleagues beyond providing direction, problem-solving, or offering advice. Rich conversations can spark more creativity and innovation in your teams and inspire a deeper level of motivation and understanding.

Unfortunately, there's no simple trick for getting better at having the kinds of deeper conversations that build connection and trust; it takes time, energy, intentionality, consistency, and practice. But there are techniques, many of which come from coaching, that you can use to improve the quality of your conversations to make them more meaningful and enjoyable.

THE ROLE OF COACHING IN ORGANIZATIONS

In over 50 years, CCL's executive coaches have coached tens of thousands of leaders. In that time, we have studied the art and practice of coaching through the onboarding and evaluation of hundreds of coaches, which helped us learn what it takes to be an exceptional coach. In turn, we have taken that knowledge to facilitate coach training skills programs for thousands of HR professionals, managers, and leaders. Our experiences have exposed us to countless life-changing, transformational conversations. As a result, we have a strong belief that better conversations will always be rooted coaching.

Coaching is a nebulous term, so it is perhaps useful to understand CCL's definition as a starting point: "A relationship between an experienced helping professional (the coach) and a leader, where the coach supports the growth and development of the leader through a series of thought-provoking and action-oriented 1-1 conversations. As part of the coaching process, the coach works with the leader to assess and understand their development needs, challenge current constraints while exploring new possibilities, and ensure accountability and support for reaching goals" (Frankovelgia & Riddle, 2010).

Formal coaching in organizations (commonly known as executive coaching) is an incredibly useful tool for both individuals and organizations, and it can help leaders have confidential conversations to make important changes in behavior and mindset, achieve higher performance, and have greater satisfaction at work (Steinberg, 2020). More than 70 percent of leadership development programs include coaching because it increases leaders' self-awareness, accelerates learning, facilitates the development of critical thinking skills, improves team leadership performance, and can lead to sustainable organizational change (Stawiski, Sass, & Belzer, 2016).

COACHING IS DIFFERENT FROM OTHER SUPPORTING RELATIONSHIPS

When most of us think about coaching, it likely conjures up helping types of behaviors, such as giving feedback, offering advice, listening, challenging, and supporting. While there are many similarities to other ways of helping, coaching is different. To understand the brilliance of using coaching skills in everyday conversations, we want you to appreciate the differences between the many types of supporting relationships familiar to us (Figure 1).

FIGURE 1. SUPPORT RELATIONSHIPS

Coaching Compared to Other Roles

	Mentoring	Sponsorship	Consulting	Counseling	Coaching
Looks Like	Advice giving	Advocacy for your career	Offers solutions	Analyzing why/ looks at the past	Asks you questions to generate insights
When Best to Use	When you need a roadmap from someone who has done it before, been in your shoes	When you need an advocate with a lot of influence for your career advancement	When needing best practices/holistic ideas of how to tackle business problems	When you need to unpack things from the past that are influencing you still today	When you need to develop and grow or deepen self-awareness

- **Mentoring.** This type of relationship typically involves a more experienced, seasoned professional (mentor) and someone who wants to learn from that person (mentee). Mentors share their experience and expertise, and give helpful advice relative to what the mentee wants to learn or do in their career. A mentor can be extremely helpful when you need a roadmap from someone who has done what you're trying to do or has been in your shoes.

- **Sponsorship.** Though similar to mentoring, sponsorship differs in that the mentor (or sponsor) also helps advocate for your career by getting you visibility on projects and with senior executives, opening doors or facilitating opportunities for your professional development, and influencing an organization on your behalf. This type of relationship is useful when you need an advocate with significant organizational influence for your career development or advancement.

- Consulting. A consultant offers solutions to specific problems or challenges. Consultants often have educational backgrounds or specialized credentials that allow them to support their clients with industry best practices as well as expertise from a diversity of client experience to tackle business problems.

- Counseling. Although coaching has some similarities with counseling, it is distinctly different. Counseling largely focuses on the past and is predicated on a medical or clinical model; it can be used to treat trauma, dysfunction, or addiction. This can be a critical supportive relationship if situations or emotions from your past are influencing your current attitude, behavior, and mindset.

Unlike the types of supportive relationships described above, coaching is largely about listening in a nonjudgmental way, asking questions to help someone generate their own insights, challenging someone's way of thinking, providing feedback in the moment, and helping create accountability so the person can achieve their goals.

To keep things simple, you can define the way you communicate at work across a continuum that ranges from directive (telling) conversation on one side, to developmental (asking) conversations on the other side (Figure 2). In between

FIGURE 2. BEHAVIOR CONTINUUM—DIRECTIVE TO DEVELOPMENTAL CONVERSATIONS

| Telling | Problem Solve | Give Advice | Make Suggestions | Provide Feedback | Challenge Thinking | Listen | Asking |

Directive Conversation   Developmental Conversation

these two opposites are a range of behaviors. All of these are important, especially in management and leadership. You likely leverage all these behaviors across the continuum—maybe even in the same conversation—but where do you think you spend most of your time? When we ask this question during our coach training programs, most people agree they spend most of their time telling or directing people what to do, problem-solving, giving advice, and making suggestions. In many ways, that makes sense. Many of these behaviors earn individual contributors the title of "high potential" in organizations. If you're someone who can solve a problem, get a project back on track with your ability to direct a team, or make suggestions that drive results, you are likely to be promoted into management.

The behaviors on the directive side of the spectrum aren't bad—they're essential for running profitable businesses. They're also incredibly useful in specific situations. Think about the last time you started a job in a new company, a new role in a different department, or were simply asked to learn a new task. Having people provide directions, suggestions, and recommendations was likely critical to your success in those situations. However, directive behaviors become problematic when they're the *only* behaviors used or when the style with which they're used has a negative impact.

If you are always there to problem-solve, it can be hard for others to learn how to solve their own challenges and develop mental maps for solving future issues. As you move up the leadership pipeline, it will become likely much more important to be able to listen to the people and teams you lead and ask the right questions to fully understand problems and help guide toward solutions rather than jump in to solve problems yourself.

Jeff Weiner joined LinkedIn in December 2008 and grew the organization from 338 to more than 16,000 employees in over 30 offices around the world. In an interview with Reed Hoffman (*Blitzscaling 19*, 2015), Weiner talked about how he was able scale the organization in such a dynamic way. A core part of this effort was to upgrade leadership through coaching skills by embracing a framework that started with problem-solving on one side of a continuum and coaching on the other. He noted that the best way to scale his team's leadership capabilities was to enable them to understand the importance of coaching. Weiner suggested that while a natural response to growth is to "knee-jerk to the aptitude of solving problems," the better approach is to evolve along the problem-solving and coaching continuum and recognize that "you need to start coaching others to solve their own problems" to achieve real scale at the leadership level. By following this continuum, you get the benefit of time to think more proactively and strategically about your business. "If you are not carving out the time to think proactively, you are not going to be effective in leading the organization, because you are going to be constantly firefighting and reacting. Taking the time to start to think ahead, as opposed to playing catch up with your competitors, is essential, because once you start playing catch up it's basically game over."

WHAT IS THE IMPACT OF USING COACHING SKILLS?

By effectively leveraging coaching skills, leaders can inspire employees, create positive learning experiences, and maximize the potential of their teams. Google's Project Oxygen gathered and analyzed data on the characteristics of their highest-performing managers and found they were all good coaches and expressed interest in and concern for team members' success and well-being (Bryant, 2011). There are also several other possible outcomes when coaching is part of an organization's leadership methodology:

- **Better and accelerated learning.** When employees receive and react constructively to feedback and coaching, they're more likely to develop learning agility, which is about knowing *how* to learn and knowing what to do when you don't know what to do, learning from experience and applying it in new ways, and adapting to new circumstances and opportunities. This ultimately allows them to be open-minded and responsive to data (Mankins & Garton, 2017, p. 104).

- **Development of critical thinking skills.** It is almost impossible to develop one's own decision-making schemas and critical thinking skills when someone constantly tells you what to do. When managers use coaching skills, they can assess when an employee needs direction and when they need space to wrestle through an issue or challenge themselves. Coaching also allows managers to focus on an employee's professional development from a skill set perspective to challenge them to gain necessary skills to achieve goals.

- Build trust. When you consistently demonstrate you care about having better conversations and developing people, you build trust in relationships—especially when you demonstrate these skills to everyone you work with, from individual contributors to peers to your superiors. It shows you value strong relationships and treating people fairly.

- Psychological safety. Over the years, Google has applied its skill at mining data to better understand what's at the core of effective leaders and teams. The top finding of their Project Aristotle was that a shared feeling of psychological safety was the most distinguishing characteristic of effective teams at Google (Duhigg & Graham, 2016). Team members who perceived a high level of psychological safety within the team showed a willingness to be vulnerable and open with one another, and this in turn encouraged sharing ideas and taking risks. Using coaching skills in conversations can model vulnerability but also create safe spaces for people to disagree, give each other hard feedback, and challenge one's thinking.

- Leadership development. Demonstrating these skills can be helpful for your own career development. Data from 1,852 leaders showed that leaders who effectively demonstrated the four core coaching behaviors (i.e., listen, ask powerful questions, challenge and support, and establish next steps and accountability) were rated significantly higher in overall leadership effectiveness by their managers than leaders who did not demonstrate these behaviors. Not only were these differences statistically significant, but they also had moderate to large effect sizes (Raper, 2019).

HOW DID THE FOUR CORE SKILLS EVOLVE?

The four core skills described in this book evolved out of CCL's framework for coaching: Relationship, Assessment, Challenge, Support, Results (RACSR), which was developed over several decades and is based on both practical professional coaching experience with clients and adult learning research. The goal is the same whether you're a professional coach or a leader leveraging coach skills: help people be more aware of their actions and behaviors, more intentional about how they work, and, ultimately, more effective members of teams and organizations. RACSR focuses on three main principles:

- the relationship between a coach and the person being coached

- the coaching skills of assessing, challenging, and supporting

- a focus on concrete results for the person being coached

RELATIONSHIP

The coaching partnership is based on rapport, commitment, and trust (Riddle & Ting, 2006). It is served by a high level of psychological safety, where someone feels comfortable sharing, asking questions, and brainstorming out loud. This cultivates a safe environment for learning and growth (Edmonson, 2018).

ASSESSMENT

Assessment's goal is to understand strengths and development opportunities for the person being coached, and includes relevant work history, their unique qualities, as well as their organizational experience and context. Data for assessment can be collected through coaching conversations, interviews, psychological assessments (including 360-degree feedback), or observations of the person being coached.

CHALLENGE

Challenge pushes someone's thinking, helps them learn to question their limiting beliefs preventing them from progressing or advancing in their careers, and gets them to experiment with stretching into new or different behaviors or mindsets outside their comfort zone.

SUPPORT

In coaching work, assessment, challenge, and support need to be balanced. The support mechanism helps people feel safe to explore, experiment, and question current ways of thinking or behaving. Support can be encouragement, helping someone maintain motivation, facilitating conversations that create clarity about action plans, and serving as an accountability partner.

RESULTS

A key goal of coaching is to help the person being coached to achieve the results most meaningful to them. The coach is responsible for helping to track goals throughout their work together, especially as they change over time, and to hold them accountable to following through on the work.

Although RACSR is a powerful framework, it can be challenging to leverage its value, especially when someone is just learning to coach. In the last several years, we have found that simplifying RACSR to four core skills has allowed new coaches to use the skills more quickly and confidently. Anyone can use these skills—not just leaders or coaches—in any conversation to make it better.

Additionally, researchers have seen a shift toward the use of more accessible, behavior-based language, providing more opportunities to bring coaching skills into the workplace. Anthony M. Grant, in the article "The Third 'Generation' of Workplace Coaching: Creating a Culture of Quality" (2017), has noted that coaching methodologies have evolved over time, going from a structured step-by-step approach to a more conversational approach, and specifically (among other elements):

FROM	TO
Formal one-on-one conversations	Coaching as a quality conversation
Prescriptive "how to coach" models	Highly flexible and agile
Highly jargonized training material	Integrates with common organizational language

One benefit of this shift is that you can use any of the four core skills at any time, without needing to learn an entire framework. The skills become a bit like Lego™ blocks: anyone can start building with just the basic blocks, and once you master the core skills, the blocks can be assembled to create houses, mansions, and castles.

Four Core Behaviors for Better Conversations

We previously shared that successful managers and leaders tend to be skilled at directive conversations and solving problems, and organizations usually reward people who get stuff done. We also shared about the importance of having conversations that allow leaders to increase their own capacity by increasing the capabilities of their teams. Although the skills used in these developmental conversations at first seem natural and obvious, we have found that they're underdeveloped and underutilized. For a lot of us, when we first start using these skills, it feels like a very different and awkward way of talking. For that reason, we have reduced over thirty years of best practices for coaching conversations into four core, easy-to-remember skills that you will be able to quickly access "on the fly" as you practice having conversations with your colleagues at work.

The four core skills for having better conversations every day are:

- **Listen to understand** so that you can suspend your own agenda.

- **Ask powerful questions** that are open-ended and come from genuine curiosity.

- **Challenge and support** in a way that's balanced for an optimal environment of development.

- **Establish next steps and accountability** at the conclusion of every conversation.

Listen to Understand	Challenge and Support
Listen for facts, feelings, and values to deepen your understanding of what is being said.	What's in your control?
	What can you influence?
What you listen for shapes what you hear. What you hear (or don't hear) can determine your response.	What do you need to accept?
	What's the stretch goal?
Pay attention to what gets in the way for you when listening (distractions, assumptions, emotions).	What's possible?
	What will you say "no" to if you say "yes" to this?
Practice your listening skills: Show attentiveness. Summarize. Clarify. Paraphrase. Stop talking.	What support do you need?

Ask Powerful Questions	Establish Next Steps and Accountability
What would be useful for you in this conversation?	What will it give you? (to achieve this goal)
Why is this important to you?	Who can keep you accountable?
How do you feel about it?	What does your next step look like?
What are the opportunities?	What will be the impact of doing this?
What are your strengths? What's getting in the way?	How will you measure success?
What's the worst thing that can happen? The best thing?	What's your specific plan for this week? Next week?
Tell me more . . . what else?	How will I know you've done what you committed to?

Conversations rooted in core coaching skills are critical for problem-solving, productivity, culture change, and locking in business results. Our research at CCL shows that when leaders use the four core coaching skills in everyday conversations, they're rated as more effective by their superiors than those who don't.

The next sections will explore each of these skills in detail. Keep in mind that the goal is not to have the best conversations. Your goal is to practice having better conversations every day, allowing yourself some grace as you learn some (though hopefully all) of these skills at your own pace.

LISTEN TO UNDERSTAND

SELF-ASSESSMENT

I listen carefully to the ideas and suggestions of others.
☐ Rarely   ☐ Sometimes   ☐ Often

I demonstrate understanding by restating or summarizing what others say.
☐ Rarely   ☐ Sometimes   ☐ Often

I show genuine curiosity in what others say.
☐ Rarely   ☐ Sometimes   ☐ Often

I demonstrate attentiveness with eye contact and body posture.
☐ Rarely   ☐ Sometimes   ☐ Often

I put distractions aside to focus on important conversations.
☐ Rarely   ☐ Sometimes   ☐ Often

I ask questions more than give advice.
☐ Rarely   ☐ Sometimes   ☐ Often

If you responded rarely or sometimes to three or more items in this list, listening to understand might be a great skill to prioritize.

Think about the kinds of conversations you have throughout the day. Maybe you're advocating for processes, solving problems, or putting out fires. When was the last time you went into a meeting with the goal of being curious, unattached from your own agenda?

Most of us have heard good listening skills are as important as being able to communicate clearly and advocate effectively for our perspective. We might have even learned "active" listening skills in school or early on in our careers. As the phrase implies, active listening is the ability to intentionally listen and understand what someone is telling you. This is often combined with making the other person feel like they're truly being heard.

In theory, active listening sounds reasonable enough, but it's incredibly difficult to practice. In our daily lives, lots of things get in the way when we try to listen:

- Time and focus. If we're pressed for time or preoccupied with something else, we will have a hard time concentrating on what someone else is saying, even if we come with the best of intentions.

- Your own agenda. If you're advocating for something you think is more important than what the other person is telling you, even the best active listener will not be truly listening.

- Your own need to be heard. If you find yourself thinking about what to say next rather than what the speaker is saying, you're not listening.

- Your ego. You might have a black belt in active listening, but if you dislike it when someone questions your ideas or actions, you're not listening.

- Your good intentions. When people come to us with issues or challenges, we want to help and provide value. If you find yourself giving advice too soon and suggesting solutions to problems before the other person has fully explained their perspective, you're not listening.

- **Your own need to talk.** Some of us simply prefer talking over listening. It can get in the way of listening to understand.

- **Your current state.** If you're hungry, angry, or tired, it'll be an uphill battle for even the best active listener.

- **Your own biases.** Your beliefs and values can get in the way of exploring other perspectives and expanding your own.

With so many things that can get in the way of effective listening, despite our best intentions and well-practiced active listening skills, the odds are against us. Luckily, at CCL we have developed a listening "hack" that is easy to remember and practice. The key to this hack is to simply be aware of the place where you're listening from and to intentionally choose to listen from the perspective of facts, feelings, and values.

BEING AWARE OF WHERE YOU'RE LISTENING FROM

Very few people start a conversation with a blank slate in their mind, ready to fill it with everything they hear from another person. Invariably, you're already listening from a preselected perspective—you either know, guess, or anticipate what's coming. Here are some of the ways "already listening" shows up:

- **Find the flaw.** You think the other person is already wrong, which is something you do when you find yourself saying "yes, but . . ." a lot.

- **Right or wrong.** From this type of listening, you're making a judgement or a decision about what the other person is

17

telling you. You might often say "You're right" or "You're wrong" to close off any possibility for more discussion.

- The cynic. This is listening from a place where you doubt anything is possible. With this kind of listening, you might say (or think), "There's no way you are going to pull this off . . ."

- The skeptic. You're listening for "the proof" of what someone is telling you. When you ask someone "How are you going to do this?" you're in the skeptic space.

TRY THIS!

ASSIGNMENT: Blank Slate Listening

DESCRIPTION: What we listen for shapes what we hear. In our everyday lives, what we look and listen for is shaped by our preferences, context, history, and immediate conditions, such as fear, hunger, fatigue, and health. What we see and hear determines how we respond. So, consider what's possible for you if you put aside your narratives and stories and try different perspectives.

Try to take a different perspective with the people you are talking with today. Better yet, don't take a perspective at all and listen with a blank slate. How might you do that? With people you already know, trying pretending you have never met them. How does that change how you listen to them or what you are hearing? What are you curious about that might be different from what you tend to focus on? How can you put yourself in their shoes to see what they see?

- What was this experience like for you?

- How did other people react to you?

- How could listening with a blank slate impact your relationships with others?

Already listening is something we all do. Sometimes this kind of listening can save us time, but there are many situations when this type of listening will not open different perspectives or opportunities. The first part of listening to understand is to be aware of your current listening perspective. The next part requires you to shift that perspective to intentionally listen for the facts, feelings, and values the other person is sharing in the conversation.

Facts. Most of us have mastered the skill of listening for facts. Facts give us a clue to the actual situation, the people involved, and the outcomes needed. Creating a common understanding and agreement on the facts is likely where we spend most of our time in conversations. In fact, in our training courses, we conduct a simple activity where participants are asked to listen to a partner from the three different perspectives. When we ask the question "What's the easiest perspective to listen from?" almost 80 percent of leaders share that listening for the facts is the most intuitive. But listening for feelings and values can yield rich insights.

Feelings. Listening for feelings might seem like an odd way to listen. How can you "listen" for a feeling? Most of the time, feelings show up in body language, in the tone of someone's voice (are they angry, happy, sad?), and in what someone shares about how they feel about a certain situation. For those of us who prefer to only listen for facts, we might miss these important clues. When you pay attention to the emotional tone of the conversation, you might find your colleagues' unstated objections, sensible reservations, and concealed barriers—all things that can stop new initiatives.

Values. When listening for values, you're trying to understand what might be important to the other person at a level that goes beyond just the facts, regardless of the topic you're discussing. For example, you may be someone who values flexibility and is willing to do anything for a customer. If you're talking to a team member who values structure and reliability for that same customer, it is important to surface those deeper values-based differences.

Values often motivate us to act. These deep-seated beliefs and standards are not typically noticed in an everyday conversation, but understanding values will yield greater insights about why your colleagues make certain decisions. In the same training course activity mentioned earlier—where we ask leaders what perspective is easiest to listen from (and where most said facts)—we also asked them to share from which perspective did they feel most heard. This time, the overwhelming majority of participants preferred being heard from the perspectives of feelings and values. We pointed out the disconnect: although most of us spend our time at work listening for facts, the way we actually want to be heard is from the perspective of feelings and values. What's possible for you if you started to listen this way? Of course, listening to understand is not the same as listening to agree or disagree, but it will lead to a richer, more sustainable conversation and, ultimately, deeper relationships in which each party has a better understanding of what's beyond the surface of facts.

The key to listening to understand is to listen from all three perspectives equally. The next time you're in a meeting or are having an important conversation, take notes from each perspective. By the end of the conversation, you will have a deep understanding of what was said.

Keep in mind that you will have a listening preference. If you find yourself more easily listening from the perspective of facts, don't worry about capturing that one as much. You've got that one; it's automatic. Focus on your less-practiced perspectives instead, which in this case would be listening for feelings and values.

TRY THIS!

ASSIGNMENT: Make Someone Feel Like They Matter

DESCRIPTION: The best way to show someone they matter to you is to listen to them. Choose one conversation or meeting today and just listen. Practice paying attention, avoiding premature judgement, and reflecting understanding. What do you hear in terms of facts, feelings, and values? Is there someone in your life who really needs to know they matter to you? If so, practice your listening with that person. If not, any conversation today will do.

REFLECTION

- What did you notice about the quality of your listening when you went in with the intention of just listening?

- What did you notice about the other person's reaction to you?

- What do you need to stop doing, start doing, or continue doing to be a better listener?

For some of us, understanding the link between listening and what it can do for us is essential for commitment to a new skill. In a 2016 whitepaper on empathy in the workplace, Gentry, Weber, and Sadri suggested that empathic emotion was positively correlated with job performance ratings. One of the ways to develop empathic skills is by becoming a good listener. If you can learn to really hear what someone is saying and *not* saying, it becomes easier to put yourself in others' shoes and demonstrate compassion. Research has also shown a strong link between people's perceptions of a "positive listening environment" and sales metrics, which suggests that listening is an essential part of building the communication culture of a successful organization (Johnston & Reed, 2017). The perception of a "positive listening environment" has also been shown to be related to an employee's connection with and commitment to an organization (Reed, Goolsby, & Johnston, 2016).

ASK POWERFUL QUESTIONS

Though it sounds simple, there's an art and science to asking questions. The goal is to do more than create a mutual understanding about the facts. At their best, questions can help uncover insights that would not have come to light otherwise. Powerful questions can take people somewhere new—beyond their original understanding of a topic or issue.

Consider the difference between these two questions:

1. "When are you going to announce the new initiative?"

2. "How do you want your team to feel when you announce the new initiative?"

The first question will help bring everyone up to speed and the response will likely be a factual statement, such as "as soon as I get final buy-in from marketing." The second question is much more likely to spark reflection and lead to greater insights.

Here is another example:

1. "Who is your audience for the presentation?"

2. "What does success look like at the end of your presentation?"

3. "What will this presentation mean for you?"

The first question might get someone to start thinking about who the key decision-makers are and how the presentation can be adjusted accordingly—a useful planning question. However, the second question casts a much wider net and, after some deeper thinking, could lead to a much richer response. The third question goes even deeper, asking about how this presentation can impact your career or professional goals.

By asking the right questions, you have the power to expand a conversation and uncover new insights. The goal is to go to a deeper level, beyond a mere understanding of the facts, by making inquiries that stretch the other person's thinking.

A couple of years ago, in a heated conversation with a family member about a sensitive topic, I (Maggie) remember making a conscious and hard decision. Even though I was frustrated and saddened by her perspective and the conversation generally, I decided to be curious enough to ask her a question I was *sure*

I didn't want to know the answer to. The result was surprising. I didn't love hearing her perspective—and I definitely didn't agree with it—but I was able to focus on the fact that I cared about her and truly wanted to understand where she was coming from. I found myself really listening to what she was saying—and not saying—and trying harder than I had before to put myself in her shoes. The more I stayed open and curious, the more I was able to ask meaningful questions and hear how much concern and fear were behind her words. As the conversation continued, I could hear her getting less and less defensive. She started sharing how she felt and revealing things I knew were uncomfortable for her. She even started asking me questions about how I saw the situation and how previous conversations had impacted me. By the end, we weren't in full agreement, but we had moved forward in a small way together. That one conversation changed the way we talk to each other, still to this day. Hard conversations don't necessarily get easier, but by using some simple techniques, they can get better.

TIPS FOR ASKING POWERFUL QUESTIONS

As you saw from the previous examples, a good, powerful question can be thought-provoking rather than thought-providing. Pay attention to how you're phrasing the question, starting with the very first word.

If you were to rank-order the words below, which would make a more powerful word to use to begin a question?

- Where
- When
- Who
- How

- Why
- What
- Which

To avoid getting yes/no answers, don't start questions with "which" as they will often be the least thought-provoking and powerful. "Who," "when," and "where" questions will also typically yield one-word answers, whereas questions starting with "what" and "how" are usually the most effective in terms of getting a deeper, more thoughtful response. Notice how in the previous example questions, the second, more powerful questions started with either "what" or "how." "What" questions get us to describe an issue, whereas "how" questions make us think about the actions that are required to make something happen.

The most powerful questions often start with "why." A "why" question, when properly used, can get to a root cause or enable us to shift perspectives. But just as it is the most powerful, a "why" question can also become the least effective if it is not set up the right way. Starting a conversation with a question like "Why did you make that decision?" will put someone on the defensive. Rather than opening new possibilities, the conversation will devolve into justifications and rationalizations.

TRY THIS!

ASSIGNMENT: Learn Something You Didn't Know

DESCRIPTION: Find out something you didn't know about someone you know well. Spouses, significant others, and parents work best for this exercise, but long-time colleagues, friends, or anybody you've known for a while and with whom you have a strong relationship will also work. The most obvious question to get this conversation started is: "Tell me something I don't know about you?"

You may come up with better (less obvious) ways to get at that information—and if you do, we would love to hear from you! Tweet or post on social media with the hashtag #CCLPowerfulQuestions.

- What was this experience like for you?

- How did the other person react to you?

- How could setting an intention to find out something you didn't know impact your relationships with others?

THE RIGHT WAY TO ASK QUESTIONS

Intent and tone matter when you ask questions. If a question like "Why did you make that decision?" is asked with genuine curiosity, the response will likely be much more introspective than if it were asked with a sense of arrogance. Approaching questions as a curious observer who wants to learn more helps us avoid trying to solve the other person's problem and will stop us from looking for the "right" answer that we want to hear or offer. When you find yourself asking a lot of leading questions ("Did you . . . have you . . .?"), you're likely in problem-solving mode. In that kind of situation, ask yourself: Is this question for my benefit or for the other person's benefit?

EXAMPLES OF POWERFUL QUESTIONS

- "What would be useful for you in this conversation?"

- "Why is this important to you?"

- "How do you feel about it?"

- "What are the opportunities?"

- "What are your strengths? What's getting in the way?"

- "What's the worst thing that can happen? The best thing?"

- "Tell me more . . . what else?"

ASSIGNMENT: Ask Yourself Powerful Questions

DESCRIPTION: Even though asking "why" can be a powerful question, it can sometimes get in the way if you're trying to focus the conversation on what you can control or influence. This has changed the way we think about feedback. Instead of asking ourselves "Why did I get this score on a program evaluation?" you can ask "What is it about this rating that matters to me?" or "What can I do with this information?" The second and third questions are far more empowering than the first.

In a deeper sense, when we ask "why," we ruminate endlessly about stuff that we can't solve. "What" and "how" questions, on the other hand, help us move forward.

This little word swap is a concept explored by the organizational psychologist Dr. Tasha Eurich, who found that the most self-aware people are those whose introspective thinking centers on questions of "what" rather than "why." But, uh, why is that?

Studies have shown that asking ourselves "why" when introspecting can cause us to ruminate on negative feelings and emotions to the point that we fill in the blanks with reasoning that can lead us away from true insight. But when we ask ourselves "what" questions, we can more easily "stay objective, future-focused and empowered to act on our new insights," Eurich writes.

For example, when you're thinking of a situation that caused you to feel bad at work, you might automatically ask yourself, "Why do I feel so terrible?" However, a better way to approach the situation would be to ask yourself, "What situations made me feel terrible, and what do they have in common?"

RESOURCES

https://www.nytimes.com/2018/01/08/smarter-living/dont-let-a-lack-of-self-awareness-hold-you-back.html

RESEARCH ON THE POWER OF ASKING QUESTIONS

Though understudied in formal research, anecdotally it is clear that asking powerful questions can be helpful— and at times even transformational—in conversations. Thankfully, research is starting to catch up and support individual experience. One study showed that people who ask more questions in conversations are better liked. The findings translate outside of work as well to show that speed daters who asked more questions were more likely to secure a second date (Huang, Yeomans, Brooks, Minson, & Gino, 2017). A second experiment conducted by the same research team, specifically looking at open-ended questions paired with attentive listening, showed that it fueled motivation by conveying to the person that they had control, competence, and that they belonged (Huang, Yeomans, Brooks, Minson, & Gino, 2017).

CHALLENGE AND SUPPORT

Both personally and professionally, people conquer their stretch goals when they feel supported. In everyday conversations, you can show your support by listening to understand and asking powerful questions. These skills give people the assurance that they've been heard and that you understand their feelings and values. However, listening and asking good questions does not always move a situation forward. A conversation in which you are heard and understood might make you feel better about your situation in some cases, but at other times you might wonder if you sound like a broken record, repeating the same "story" without any kind of breakthrough or resolution.

Having better conversations often includes helping each other explore new possibilities by challenging baseline thinking and assumptions. Think about a time when someone said something or asked you a question that completely changed the way you thought about something. It's human, but we often get locked into certain ways of seeing things and assume we have all the answers. Then, if someone comes up with the right question, it can completely change how we see the situation. We have one client who introduced better conversations to their entire organization and commented, "We are getting better at open-ended questions and are getting to better answers because of it." When we challenge and support, we provide opportunities to see outside of the limits of our current way of thinking but do so in a way that permits us to take measured, achievable risks.

What does challenge and support look like in a conversation? One way is to ask tough questions that stress-test a person's ideas and uncover their unexamined assumptions. Examples of challenging questions include:

- "What are you afraid of?"

- "What's the worst thing that could happen?"

- "If you couldn't be fired, what might you try?"

Another way is to increase a person's self-awareness through a question:

- "Why does this matter to you as much as it does?"

- "What's in your control?"

- "What can you influence?"

- "What do you need to accept?"

- "What's possible?"

- "What's missing?"

- "What will you say 'no' to if you say 'yes' to this?"

ASSIGNMENT: Challenge Your Own Story

DESCRIPTION: The next time you are feeling frustrated with someone, ask yourself:

1. "What did this person actually do to frustrate me?"

2. "What is the story I'm making up about what that behavior means?"

3. "Is it the behavior or my interpretation of the behavior that causes my frustration?"

Then, have a conversation with that person about the behavior, the impact their behavior had on you, and what they intended by the behavior.

- What was the experience like?

- What did you notice about the other person's reaction to you?

- What might be the value of challenging your story more often?

PROVIDING FEEDBACK

I provide timely, positive feedback.
☐ Rarely ☐ Sometimes ☐ Often

I provide timely, constructive feedback.
☐ Rarely ☐ Sometimes ☐ Often

I give feedback in the moment.
☐ Rarely ☐ Sometimes ☐ Often

I help others understand the impact of their actions.
☐ Rarely ☐ Sometimes ☐ Often

I help others understand the intent and if their impact matches.
☐ Rarely   ☐ Sometimes   ☐ Often

If you responded "rarely" or "sometimes" to three or more items, feedback might be a good place to focus some of your leadership energy.

Feedback is one of the best ways to challenge and support others. Most people assume that feedback is just being told that you did a good or bad job on a task, but researchers have found that feedback is also about *how* you do something—your style, the way you communicate, the way people feel about interacting with you (Medvedeff, Gregory, & Levy, 2008). The way you show up or behave can have either the impact you intended or the opposite effect, where what you intended does not create the desired impact at all. In this context, feedback is about uncovering the potential difference between your impact and intent. You might have a desired intention, but the way it shows up in your behavior could have an entirely different impact on the other person. For example, suppose I (Andre) have been working on a key project that has been taking most of my time in the last month. I haven't been getting back to people on time and have been delaying decisions on key items. I notice that my boss is starting to make decisions on my behalf and is responding to emails on which she has been copied. I could easily start making up stories about the intention behind my boss's behavior: she doesn't trust me, she thinks I don't know what I'm doing, she's micromanaging, and so on.

I could go to my boss and say, "I don't think you trust me," or "I noticed you've been micromanaging me." We all know how these conversation starters might go. My boss would likely get defensive or shut down, and our conversation wouldn't go anywhere—all because I am leading with my own interpretation of the intent behind her behavior.

Successful feedback fixes this disconnect between impact and intent. My boss's behavior is the part I see—that's the impact. But the thoughts, feelings, and meaning behind the behavior are below the surface—that's the intent. If I want to have a better conversation, it's important that I first talk with her about the behavior that is bothering me, share the impact that behavior has had on me, and only then inquire about her intent.

There is a useful, easy-to-remember formula to frame this feedback conversation: SBI.

S Situation
Grounded in time and place

B Behavior
Physical, observable action

I Impact
What I felt/ thought/did

Let's see how this might play out with my boss:

Situation: "Several times over the last few months . . ."

Behavior: "You have made decisions about things within my area of responsibility without consulting me or communicating them to me. For example, you responded to both John and Sandra's emails about what we intended to do about the project before I could respond. You also told the design group we were deprioritizing our review process before talking to me about that decision."

Impact: "I'm concerned this undermines my authority with my team and communicates a lack of trust."

If I deliver this feedback and then pause, it gives my boss a chance to respond. Maybe she responds by saying, "Oh, I didn't realize I was doing that, I just know how busy you have been. Let's talk about your responsibility versus mine." That would allow us to then move toward discussing a solution. On the other hand, my boss might respond by saying, "Yes, I'm glad you brought this up. I'm making those decisions because I've become increasingly less confident in your ability to make good decisions." Tough feedback, but good to know because now we know what the conversation needs to be about. We could then continue the conversation by asking, "Can you help me understand more about what's going on?" and learn more about her intention. Either way, good or bad, I am getting information that I need to make decisions moving forward, and we're on to a better conversation.

The same formula can be used to "support" behavior that had or is having a positive impact on you. Have you ever given or received a compliment that fell flat, was awkward, or just didn't seem sincere? Sometimes it's necessary to express sincere appreciation for something someone did or is doing that's having a positive impact on us. SBI can be the formula that turns that conversation from awkward to productive. Let's look at an example.

A while back, I was on call with a client that wasn't going well. The client would ask questions and start complaining before I could even get my answer out. This went on for a while, and I was getting increasingly frustrated when my colleague jumped in and asked the client, "What's your goal in this conversation?" The client paused, answered the question, and their entire demeanor changed. From that point on, we asked questions and listened to understand. In the end, the client was happy and excited about moving forward. Now, after the call, I could have just said "nice job" to my colleague and that would have been that. But their behavior had a bigger impact on me than that. They reminded me of the power of asking questions and really listening. So, my supportive feedback to them was:

> Situation: "During the call with client XYZ last Monday . . ."

> Behavior: "Thank you for jumping in when you did. I was feeling attacked and frustrated so your timing was perfect. I especially appreciate how you led with a powerful question and just listened."

> Impact: "You reminded me of the power of asking questions and listening and I was both grateful and impressed."

ASSIGNMENT: Catch Someone Doing Something Right

DESCRIPTION: Every day, people all around us are doing things we appreciate, yet it's rare that we take the time to express our appreciation. Today is going to be different. Today's task is to specifically look for what's *right* about what others are doing. Notice even the little things that you appreciate in what others are doing, even if it's something that person does every day and you've learned to take it for granted. Then, before the end of the day, give at least one person a positive SBI to communicate your appreciation.

REFLECTION

- What was the experience like?

- What did you notice about the other person's reaction to you?

- What might be the value of expressing appreciation more often?

FEEDBACK RESEARCH

Although there is debate in the research community about the magic ratio of positive-to-constructive feedback (Gottman, 1994; Zenger & Folkman, 2013), CCL assumes that leaders need to provide both positive and constructive feedback, with an emphasis on positive feedback. And there are a couple good reasons for that. First, if every feedback conversation your boss had with you was about what you were doing wrong, you would learn over time to dread those conversations and wouldn't necessarily look at feedback as an opportunity to course correct, grow, or learn. Second, the brain may actually struggle with hearing constructive feedback. Researcher Naomi Eisenberger out of University of California, Los Angeles has shown that the area in the brain activated when you get physically hurt, like a sunburn, is the same area triggered when you get your feelings hurt. Constructive feedback—even if true and necessary to hear—can hurt, and your brain might process it the same as if you got punched in the stomach (Eisenberger & Lieberman, 2004). This means we need to both get better at giving hard feedback and become more resilient to hearing it so we can move past our brain's first response and decide how to leverage the new information. When people hear more positive than negative, it can help them trust the person's intentions because more conversations are about catching that person doing something well. When the time comes for harder conversations, it may be easier to want to do something about it.

Gentry and Young (2017) showed that managers who demonstrated courage and skill in providing challenging feedback were rated as more promotable by their bosses. This is great news for those leaders and the organizations they support. A 2018 global study of 234 organizations jointly conducted by the Center for Effective Organizations (CEO) and the Institute for Corporate Productivity (I4CP) revealed establishing a strong performance feedback culture was a predictor of corporate financial performance. Companies that scored in the top third of their performance feedback culture indicator had double the results in net profit margin compared with the lower third of companies.

How can you help feedback conversations become better conversations? Research from 2017 showed that displaying empathic concern (saying things like, "I really want you to succeed in this role . . ." or "I recognize how hard you're working and how challenging this is . . .") coupled with constructive feedback can increase positive emotional reactions to negative feedback. Additionally, empathic concern combined with high-quality, constructive feedback predicted leader promotability as evaluated by bosses (Young et al., 2017). Main takeaway: positive emotions like enthusiasm, hope, and interest can motivate employees to act on negative feedback. Being recognized as capable of doing this well can also help you in your career.

It may also be helpful to consider timing when giving feedback. One of CCL's lowest-rated items in the CCL 360 competency suite is "the ability to give timely feedback." Best practice is to give positive feedback as quickly as possible, while people are doing things right to help them understand what to keep doing, which will help you build up that positive feedback "bank account." When giving constructive feedback, you want to wait long enough so you aren't leading with your emotions (if you have ever sent an ALL-CAPS email about something you were frustrated about, you know what I am talking about)—but you also want to provide timely feedback so the person has an opportunity to reflect on and correct the issue before it becomes a bigger performance issue. If your direct report is learning about an issue or behavior concern at their annual performance review, it's already too late. People need a chance to course correct. A long-time CCL coach, Jordan Goldrich, in the book *Workplace Warrior*, says not giving someone constructive feedback is like letting someone you're talking to walk backward off a cliff without saying anything. Not sharing concerns or raising issues about behavior or performance is akin to letting someone slowly fail without giving them a chance to do something about it.

Beyond providing clear, meaningful feedback that describes the situation, behavior, and impact, another way to challenge and support is by asking powerful questions. Recall that good, powerful questions are open, not leading, concise, and generally start with "what" or "how." Challenging and supporting questions are no different in that regard. The difference is that challenge and support questions are targeted to help others see beyond the limits of their current thinking and to show the other person you're committed to their success. Another way for you to know you're asking a challenging question specifically is that it will feel different. Whereas a regular powerful question often come from a place of curiosity, a challenging question will come from a place of courageousness. Some of these questions can be life changing.

Tope Awotona is the founder and CEO of Calendly, a scheduling tool that eliminates the back and forth of emailing to set a meeting. Tope grew up in Nigeria and moved to the United States when he was a teenager. Deep down, he always wanted to become a successful entrepreneur and so spent years trying to build various businesses. After three failed attempts, Tope realized he was just focused on ways to make money. So, he asked himself, "What's a problem I am truly passionate about solving?" It took another year before he found that problem. He'd spent a day wasting a lot of time going back and forth over email to schedule meetings and noticed most scheduling programs were slow and clunky. So, he asked another powerful question: "What if I could create a better way of scheduling meetings?" After months of research, he decided to go all in with his idea. He put every single dollar he had made into this new business. In 2021, Tope's company had around $30 million in annual revenue and over 4 million users (Khan, n.d.).

TIPS FOR ASKING CHALLENGING AND SUPPORTING QUESTIONS

Ask "why" and "if" questions. Asking "why" challenges us to dig deeper to find the true purpose behind our convictions and it challenge assumptions that keep us locked into certain limiting ways of thinking. "Why does it work this way?" or "Why is that your goal?" or "Why not?" are just a few assumption-challenging "why" questions. Asking "if" questions pushes us in the direction of more possibilities. "You say you can't do this. What would it look like if you could?" or "If you had nothing to lose, what would you do?"

Be playful and provocative. Playful and provocative questions force us to think of possibilities we never would have allowed ourselves to consider. "If you had a magic wand, what would you do?" or "If you were 80 years old (or eight), how would you look at this?" These types of questions take us out of the confines of our current reality to imagine what else might be possible.

Focus on the person, not the problem. When someone comes to us with a problem, the first thing we typically want to do is solve it for them. And yet, if we really want a conversation to be developmental, we must help them solve their own problem. We do this by asking questions that challenge the thinking of the other person and help them see more possibilities. One way to think about focusing on the person is to ask "solution-finding" questions rather than problem-solving questions. For example, a problem-solving question might sound like: "Have you tried the fix we used last time for this problem?" versus a solution-finding question,

FOCUS ON THE PROBLEM	FOCUS ON THE PERSON
Asking about the problem so you can solve the challenge for the individual.	Asking questions so the person can solve their own problem.
Focus of questions is all about the problem.	Focus of questions goes beyond the details of the problem and explores more about the person.
Questions tend to be more tactical and surface level.	Questions tend to be more strategic and go deeper into what matters most.
Example: What time does the presentation start?	Example: What impact do you want your presentation opening to have on the group?
Example: How many hours a week do you work?	Example: How sustainable is your pace?
Example: What does your boss do that is frustrating you?	Example: What impact does your boss have on you?

which might sound like: "What have you tried so far? What was useful in the past? What's a different way of looking at this?"

Hold up a mirror. Holding up a mirror means we challenge and support others by helping them see themselves in the moment. For example, if you notice a shift in facial expression or body language that appears to have been precipitated by a thought or feeling, you can ask something like "Your facial expression changed. What just happened?"

Goal of support. Supporting others in a better conversation shows you're committed to and invested in the success of the person you're talking to and ensures they have identified the resources and support they need to achieve their goals. Note that it takes the right balance (a maximum amount of challenge and support), and this might not necessarily feel comfortable.

OTHER EXAMPLES OF CHALLENGE AND SUPPORT QUESTIONS

- "Where have you seen something like this before?"

- "What's the cost of not making a change?"

- "How might others view this situation?"

- "What alternatives might you imagine?"

- "What might get in your way of being successful?"

- "When you think about being successful, how does it feel?"

- "What resources do you need and how will you get them?"

GET THE BALANCE RIGHT

Experiencing maximum challenge along with maximum support will yield the most effective conversations and, in turn, will likely create powerful changes in a person's life. Picture a mountain climber. You might visualize someone perched high on a precipitous ledge. It all might look very risky until you look closer and see this person is tethered to ropes anchored solidly into the mountain. You might also notice a look of exhilaration on the person's face. They're in full control as they step outside their comfort zone—while fully supported. If you want to effectively challenge in a conversation, you need good support structures in place. If you have built a relationship authentically by listening to understand and showing genuine curiosity, then you already have a great foundation for support.

We previously discussed some of the research on feedback and how challenging and supporting with feedback can be a useful tool for leaders and organizations. Research is also clear that all types of support can be important for the perception of leadership potential and performance. A study of 598 managers who participated in CCL programs showed that managers who got higher ratings on supportiveness from their direct reports also received higher ratings on performance and promotability from their bosses (Paustian-Underdahl et al., 2013).

ESTABLISH NEXT STEPS AND ACCOUNTABILITY

Conversations should always have a clear next step; it doesn't matter if the next step is big or small. The next step could range from "I'm going to think about this" to "I'm going to take the job and move my entire life to another country." This step should always be grounded in accountability. When you create the next steps, you're taking what, at that moment, is conceptual and turning it into something real. For example, exercise might be very important to you, but you have realized you're sacrificing the time you need to stay fit and using it to work instead. After a series of challenging conversations, it becomes clear you need to reclaim some of this time and you resolve to adjust your schedule. This works for about two weeks, after which you move back into your old habits. What happened? Your next step wasn't real enough. So how do you make it real?

- **Be specific about *what*.** What exactly are you going to do? What does it look like? Do you prefer going to the gym? Riding a bike? Running, swimming, or walking?

- **Be specific about *when* and *where* and for *how long*.** At what time each day are you going to exercise? How much time are you scheduling? Where will you be?

- **Measure.** The scientist William Thompson Kelvin, famous for the Kelvin measurement unit of absolute temperatures, is purported to have said, "When you can measure what you are speaking about, and express it in numbers, you know something about it" (Ratcliffe, 2016). Having a benchmark for what you're striving to achieve is a helpful tool for goal achievement.

- **A deep connection.** Remind yourself about your why. Perhaps the deeper meaning for your desire to exercise is that your health is important for both you and your family.

- **Big goal, small steps.** Making it real doesn't mean you should hold back on achieving a big goal. It's better to start with a stretch goal that really excites you versus a goal that is more achievable. At the same time, keep in mind that it's a journey.

- **Accountability.** Even if we have the best intention to follow through, we don't. This is where having an accountability partner can make a huge difference. In fact, research shows that if you set a goal and write it down, you have about a 30 percent chance of achievement. However, if you set a goal, write it down, and share it with an accountability partner, your chances of follow through increase to a whopping 85 percent or higher (Locke & Latham, 1985).

- Focus on what you can control. So often what we try to do seems overwhelming and out of our control. It's helpful to categorize what you need to accept, what you can influence, and only worry about what you can control. You might be able to influence your schedule so that you have time to exercise early in the morning. Or, if you have family obligations, it might mean accepting that you have three days a week to work out. But the time you do have is fully in your control. At the end of any discussion about next steps, both parties should walk away with a shared understanding of what they discussed so that important insights and decisions aren't lost. You can be sure everybody feels a sense of accountability by establishing the next steps.

Often, conversations tackle complex challenges with no "right" answer. In these cases, declare one small next step that will move the issue forward. For example, "I'll let you know how the meeting goes tomorrow." Or "Will you send me an email with the document we discussed?" Committing to this follow-up shows your support for the other person and demonstrates that you value the facts and emotions they shared.

TRY THIS!

ASSIGNMENT: Giving Advice

DESCRIPTION: Feel the urge to give advice? Here's how to leverage it in a better way.

As you read above, listening to understand can be more effective than giving advice and trying to solve someone's problem. But what if it's so obvious that the other person just needs to be told what to do? There's a way to give advice, so don't be surprised that it involves listening, asking questions, challenging and supporting, and establishing next steps.

Step 1: Start by just listening to understand. People often ask for advice when they really just want to feel heard. Asking a question like "How can I be most helpful to you in this conversation?" can help focus the discussion. Support by repeating back what you heard so you create a common understanding.

Step 2: Then, consider if you are the right person to provide advice. Do you have knowledge or expertise that can help? If yes, check to see if it's useful for the other person to hear. If not, identify other people who could help.

Step 3: Collaborate and brainstorm on potential ideas together. Make sure it's not a one-way conversation and there are equal amounts of asking and telling. Challenge and support with questions like "How can we work on this together?" or "What will this approach give you?"

Step 4: Finally, end with a next step that focuses on what's best for the other person (not you). Summarize the takeaways and don't be attached to ensuring that all of your advice is accepted. Ask: "Which of these suggestions resonated with you most?"

Next time you feel the urge to blurt out some (excellent!) advice, keep these steps in mind.

- "What will it give you (to achieve this goal)?"

- "Who can keep you accountable?"

- "What does your next step look like?"

- "What will be the impact of doing this?"

- "How will you measure success?"

- "What's your specific plan for this week? Next week?"

- "How will I know you've done what you committed to?"

RESEARCH ON NEXT STEPS AND ACCOUNTABILITY

There's no shortage of articles on the best ways to set goals, and there's some compelling research about why goal setting can be impactful. Goal setting has additional benefits beyond helping you achieve what you're aiming for—the simple act of setting a goal also strengthens and maintains overall motivation, keeps you committed to sustainable behavior change, aligns your focus, and creates a path to greater self-mastery (Boss, 2017).

WHAT GETS IN THE WAY OF BETTER CONVERSATIONS?

Having better conversations doesn't necessarily fix all the natural challenges that come with communication. Conversations aren't a thing you perfect or solve for, but they're something you must consistently work on. Hard conversations aren't necessarily going to be less hard, but they can be more productive and help you get somewhere new. Here are some things that can get in the way of having better conversations in your life that you will benefit from managing:

EMOTIONS

Antonio Damasio (1995), a neuroscientist at University of Southern California, said, "We are not thinking machines. We are feeling machines that think." Research has shown our brains can get hijacked by emotions that can cause us to react in conversations in ways we don't intend and negatively impact both the discussion and the relationship. In the absence of data, our brains also tend to make up stories based on inaccurate interpretations of experiences. Learn to watch your own cues when you're in a conversation that isn't going well so you can reframe or take a break and come back to the conversation.

TIME

Although it may take more time on the front end to use coaching skills, using these skills to have better conversations consistently, over time, will help you work faster and resolve conflicts more easily. If you find yourself making excuses about not having time to develop these skills, experiment by asking one powerful question in a conversation or listening for something you don't tend to listen for automatically—facts, feelings, or values—with one other person.

OUR OWN NEEDS

Many times, our ego can get in the way of prioritizing better conversations. We want to control situations or advocate for our own ideas. Sometimes we believe that what we think is better, or more important, and we focus on being right more than anything else. In his book *The 7 Habits of Highly Effective People,* Stephen R. Covey famously wrote: "Seek first to understand, then to be understood." Use the listening skills you learned earlier in this guide to become aware that others' needs will be different than yours, and unless you truly listen to understand you will end up in an endless loop of misalignment and frustration.

WHAT'S POSSIBLE WHEN YOU USE THESE FOUR CORE SKILLS

We have found these skills transformational both at work and in our personal lives. We would not have been able to write this guide without asking powerful questions, listening to understand, and providing each other challenge along with support. And certainly, the phrase "what's the next step?" kept us on task. As part of the process of writing, we also collected many stories from individuals, teams, and organizations about the impact of leveraging better conversations. A few examples follow.

"JUST STOP TALKING AND LISTEN"

A president of a billion-dollar segment for a multinational Fortune 500 organization shared that practicing the four basic skills we've mentioned in this book has been impactful. Applying the skills gave him more comfort in developing closer/intimate relationships with people. Specifically, "I am a big extrovert, and I keep a Post-it to remind me that sometimes I just need to stop talking and listen to understand."

"As I applied the skills, specifically when many of us worked remotely during the pandemic, I realized that having conversations was a lot more challenging because of how disconnected people felt. It was also difficult getting to next steps and that has been a critical part of my engagement with individuals and in meetings. There's meeting fatigue, so being intentional about having just one, right next step has been helpful. Intuitively, we all know that conversations should have a next step, but it didn't always happen. Being intentional about applying just that one specific skill has made our executive team better."

When you commit to using these skills for yourself, you may find that your conversations and, possibly, your entire world opens. In business, results happen at the speed of relationships. One study (Patterson et al., 2012) found that every important conversation ignored or not held well costs an organization an average of $7,500 and more than seven workdays. Think of times you've tried to get good work done with a colleague or a department who you don't have a great relationship with. My guess is that the work didn't go easily or quickly. Using these skills can help people build better relationships—not just for the sake of building relationships but to drive results and execution. These skills can also help you connect with people outside of work. Think about how listening to and having a deeper understanding of your family, neighbors, and close friends might change the quality of those relationships. What might be possible if you could talk about things you don't agree on?

"THE ENTIRE TEAM NEEDED TO WORK TOGETHER"

Key groups inside of a major university we worked with struggled with inconsistent performance management conversations and a general lack of feedback from managers. We decided on a basic guiding principle: good conversations are not only the responsibility of managers and leaders. Rather, the entire team needed to work together to have good conversations.

The university reported back to us that the teams began to tackle problems by asking open-ended questions before jumping into problem-solving; managers were coaching each other on tricky conversations; and feedback from the team showed increased accountability, enhanced engagement, and signals that more effective conversations were happening every day. "If you don't fix the conversations, then it really doesn't matter what the process looks like," said the university's director of HR strategy and effectiveness.

The power of better conversations is in scaling them across organizations, and beyond. We believe these skills are going to change the way you think about your interactions with people and strengthen and deepen the relationships you care about. If you share these skills with people—your teams, your direct reports, your family—you're reinforcing your own skill set, learning, and teaching others, which creates an impact far bigger than you alone could have. Imagine if everyone in your life started to use these four core skills—creating a common language, understanding, and experience—what might be possible? Here are a couple of outcomes the four core skills can create for groups and teams:

- Get the best out of people. When you're engaging people in conversations by listening, asking for their input and perspective, and pushing them to think outside their own limiting beliefs, you can draw the best out in people and the best out of yourself. At scale, this can enable you to pull people together around common goals and create high-performing teams.

- Develop your direct reports. When you apply coaching skills to conversations with groups, especially direct reports, you can engender better performance, improve decision-making, and ensure your employees clearly understand their roles and how to be successful. These skills also enable better conversations about what employees want to do in their careers, what it will take to develop necessary skills, and accountability to reach specific goals.

- Improvement in team leadership performance. When teams have better conversations every day, it builds relationships and trust between and among members, and when you have relationships built on a foundation of trust, you tend to have more effective conversations—it's a virtuous cycle. When teams focus on their tasks and projects, manage and leverage their conflict and differences, and encourage each other to strengthen those connections and celebrate and replicate each other's successes, teams are capable of achieving exponentially more than the individual members themselves. That sense of accomplishment along with the high level of trust can create a feeling of belonging, which can result in better resilience and stress management during challenging times.

"BETTER CULTURE STARTS WITH BETTER CONVERSATIONS"

Conversation is the foundation for everything: more innovation, leading people through change and transition, Equity, Diversity, and Inclusion (EDI)—all are rooted in creating the conditions for psychological safety and trust through developmental and perspective-expanding conversations, which can make or break organizational success.

These kinds of conversations are a *requirement* for the "Future Leader." CCL research demonstrates that human-centered organizations are the ones that will thrive—that organizations must build the *collective* capacity of leaders to deal with ambiguity and change. Introducing these four core skills at the organizational level can fuel a human-centered organization and create an environment where people can show up as their best selves.

Over the years, CCL has worked with many organizations on large-scale culture-change initiatives. In one case, a newly formed insurance company identified that the ability to have more effective conversations was going to be the key differentiator in an incredibly competitive field. The ultimate goal was to move away from command-and-control leadership and build a flatter organization with a culture of collaborative teamwork. The company also sought to move away from annual performance reviews by using more frequent and effective feedback.

The CEO was adamant any coaching skills training should be simple and focus on core skills. An academic approach with complex models was discouraged in favor of a straightforward, practical approach that could create a coaching culture throughout the entire organization. Over the course of six months, every single employee went through a targeted program to learn and practice the four core skills. After implementing these approaches, having conversations about difficult topics became easier. One leader shared, "My manager has always been very receptive to open conversations both positive and negative, so it's nice to have this as a cornerstone of our corporate culture." Another leader shared giving and receiving frank feedback outside of a management hierarchy allowed her to feel empowered, since giving feedback was "our responsibility to do so" in their culture of better conversations.

Conversations are the most basic building blocks of any organization's culture and improving how people talk can have major implications on the overall well-being of a company culture. The culture of an organization is more powerful than the strategy and can be more persistent than the vision—it's the environment that enables performance or undermines it. The idea behind these four core skills is that better culture starts with better conversations. Designed to be simple, anyone can learn and master the skills so everyone can use them in every single conversation. When done consistently across organizations, you can improve the quality of conversations, shift the entire culture of an organization, and accelerate positive business outcomes (Ainsworth & Been, 2019).

When an entire organization shares a common understanding of these skills and concepts, it creates a living, learning laboratory. Any conversation can be an experiment in how these skills can create connection in different ways, create bridges among groups with different goals and competing priorities, and ultimately drive business outcomes and create lasting change.

It may seem silly, but conversation is one of the most powerful tools a leader can use to fundamentally change an organization from the inside out. As a top leader shared with us, "In a time when we see things in the news where folks turn a blind eye to bad behavior and disrespect, this is a very powerful concept and turning it into reality is truly a culture game-changer for us." Imagine if everyone in your organization was using these skills? What might be possible?

BIBLIOGRAPHY

Ainsworth, C., & Been, R. (2019). *Better culture starts with better conversations: How more effective conversations can transform your organization.* Retrieved from Center for Creative Leadership website: https://www.ccl.org/wp-content/uploads/2019/09/better-culture-better-conversations-center-for-creative-leadership.pdf

Blitzscaling 19: Jeff Weiner on Establishing a Plan and Culture for Scaling. (2015, December 8) [Video]. YouTube. https://www.youtube.com/watch?v=cYN3ghAam14

Boss, J. (2017, January 19). 5 reasons why goal setting will improve your focus. *Forbes.* Retrieved from https://www.forbes.com/sites/jeffboss/2017/01/19/5-reasons-why-goal-setting-will-improve-your-focus/?sh=1cb74260534a

Bryant, A. (2011, March 12). Google's quest to build a better boss. *New York Times.* Retrieved from https://www.nytimes.com/2011/03/13/business/13hire.html

Damasio, A. R. (1995). *Descartes' error: emotion, reason, and the human brain.* New York: Avon Books.

Dellaert, M., & Kernick, K. (2019). *Driving performance in financial services: Critical leadership capabilities your organization needs.* Retrieved from Center for Creative Leadership website: https://1ujri81m7rxc49yn1w1alaot-wpengine.netdna-ssl.com/wp-content/uploads/2019/02/critical-leadership-competencies-needed-in-finserv-financial-services-industry-center-for-creative-leadership.pdf

Duhigg, C., & Graham, J. (2016, February 25). What Google learned from its quest to build the perfect team. *New York Times.* Retrieved from https://www.nytimes.com/2016/02/28/magazine/what-google-learned-from-its-quest-to-build-the-perfect-team.html

Edmondson, A. C. (2018). *The fearless organization: Creating psychological safety in the workplace for learning, innovation, and growth.* Hoboken, NJ: Wiley.

Eisenberger, N. I., & Lieberman, M. D. (2004). Why rejection hurts: A common neural alarm system for physical and social pain. *TRENDS in Cognitive Science, 8*, 294–300. doi:10.1016/j.tics.2004.05.010

Frankovelgia, C. C., & Riddle, D. D. (2010). Four leadership coaching. In. E. Van Velsor, C. D. McCauley, & M. N. Ruderman (Eds.), *The Center for Creative Leadership Handbook of Leadership Development* (3rd ed., pp. 125–146). San Francisco, CA: Jossey Bass.

Gentry, W. A., Weber, T. J., & Sadri, G. (2016). *Empathy in the workplace: A tool for effective leadership*. Retrieved from Center for Creative Leadership website: https://cclinnovation.org/wp-content/uploads/2020/03/empathyintheworkplace.pdf

Gentry, W. A., & Young, S. F. (2017). *Busting myths about feedback: What leaders should know*. Retrieved from Center for Creative Leadership website: https://cclinnovation.org/wp-content/uploads/2020/02/busting-myths-about-feedback-ccl-white-paper.pdf

Gottman, J. M. (1994). *What predicts divorce?* Hillsdale, NJ: Lawrence Erlbaum Associates.

Grant, A. M. (2017). The third "generation" of workplace coaching: Creating a culture of quality conversations. *Coaching, 10*, 37–53. doi:10.1080/17521882.2016.1266005

Huang, K., Yeomans, M., Brooks, A. W., Minson, J., & Gino, F. (2017). It doesn't hurt to ask: Question-asking increases liking. *Journal of Personality and Social Psychology, 113*, 430–452. doi:10.1037/pspi0000097

Institute for Corporate Productivity and the Center for Effective Organizations. (2018). *Performance Feedback Culture Drives Business Impact*. Retrieved from the Center for Effective Organizations website: https://ceo.usc.edu/wp-content/uploads/2019/07/Performance-Feedback-Culture-Drives-Business-Performance-i4cp-CEO-002-1.pdf

Johnston, M. K., & Reed, K. (2017). Listening environment and the bottom line: How a positive environment can improve financial outcomes. *International Journal of Listening, 31*, 71–79. doi:10.108 0/10904018.2014.965391

Khan, O. (Host). (n.d.). Calendly's founder: Building a $30M SaaS after 3 failed startups (No. 213) [Audio podcast episode]. In *The SaaS Podcast*. https://saasclub.io/podcast/calendlys-founder-finding-saas-success-after-failed-startups/

Locke, E. A., & Latham, G. P. (1985). The application of goal setting to sports. *Journal of Sport Psychology, 7*, 205–222.

Mankins, M. C., & Garton, E. (2017). *Time, talent, energy: Overcome organizational drag and unleash your team's productive power*. Brighton, MA: Harvard Business Review Press.

Medvedeff, M., Gregory, J. B., & Levy, P. E. (2008). How attributes of the feedback message affect subsequent feedback seeking: The interactive effects of feedback sign and type. *Psychologica Belgica, 48*, 109–125. doi:10.5334/pb-48-2-3-109

Patterson, K., Grenny, J., McMillan, R., Switzler, A., & Covey, S. R. (2012). *Crucial conversations*, 2nd ed. New York: McGraw-Hill.

Paustian-Underdahl, S. C., Shanock, L. R., Rogelberg, S. G., Scott, C. W., Justice, L., & Altman, D. G. (2013). Antecedents to supportive supervision: An examination of biographical data. *Journal of Occupational and Organizational Psychology, 86*, 288–309. doi:10.1111/joop.12019

Raper, M. (2019). *Better Conversations Every Day Research Case*. Internal Report, Center for Creative Leadership, unpublished.

Ratcliffe, S. (Ed.). (2016). *Oxford essential quotations*. Retrieved from https://www.oxfordreference.com/view/10.1093/acref/9780191826719.001.0001/q-oro-ed4-00006236

Reed, K., Goolsby, J. R., & Johnston, M. K. (2016). Extracting meaning and relevance from work: The potential connection between the listening environment and employee's organizational identification and commitment. *International Journal of Business Communication, 53*, 326–342. doi:10.1177/2329488414525465

Riddle, D. & Ting, S. (2006). Leader coaches: Principles and issues for in-house development. *Leadership in Action, 26*, 13–18. doi:10.1002/lia.1156

Stawiski, S., Sass, M., & Belzer, R. G. (2016). *Building the case for executive coaching.* Retrieved from Center for Creative Leadership website: https://cclinnovation.org/wp-content/uploads/2020/02/building-the-case-for-executive-coaching.pdf

Steinberg, B. (2020, October 30). Are you ready to be coached? *Harvard Business Review.* Retrieved from https://hbr.org/2020/10/are-you-ready-to-be-coached?

Young, S., Richard, E., Moukarzel, R., Steelman, L., & Gentry, W. (2017). How empathic concern helps leaders in providing negative feedback: A two-study examination. *Journal of Occupational and Organizational Psychology, 90*, 535–558. 10.1111/joop.12184.

Zenger, J., & Folkman, J. (2013, March 15). The ideal praise-to-criticism ratio. *Harvard Business Review.* Retrieved from https://hbr.org/2013/03/the-ideal-praise-to-criticism

The Center for Creative Leadership (CCL)® is a top-ranked, global provider of leadership development. By leveraging the power of leadership to drive results that matter most to clients, CCL transforms individual leaders, teams, organizations, and society. Our array of cutting-edge solutions is steeped in extensive research and experience gained from working with hundreds of thousands of leaders at all levels. Ranked among the world's top providers of executive education, CCL has offices in countries worldwide.

Printed in the USA
CPSIA information can be obtained
at www.ICGtesting.com
LVHW060048230224
772606LV00069B/1784